Bull Sharks

Victoria Blakemore

vblakemore.author@gmail.com

Copyright info/picture credits

Cover, studio5050/AdobeStock; Page 3, Krzysztof Bargiel / AdobeStock; Page 5, Harry Collins/AdobeStock; Page 7, Tomas/AdobeStock; Page 9, Nadeen/Adobestock; Pages 10-11, peangdao/AdobeStock; Page 13, Mark Kostich/AdobeStock; Page 15, Valentina/AdobeStock; Page 17, Tomas/ AsobeStock; Page 19, Griffin/AdobeStock; Page 21, Carlos Grillo/AdobeStock; Page 23; prochym/AdobeStock; Page 25, Elise/AdobeStock; Page 27, Sahara Frost/AdobeStock; Page 29, Thomas/AdobeStock; Page 31, subphoto/AdobeStock; Page 33, studio5050/AdobeStock

Table of Contents

What Are Bull Sharks?

Bull sharks are large fish. They are related to other sharks such as great whites and tiger sharks.

Bull sharks are **apex predators**. They do not have any natural **predators** and help to balance the **ecosystem** they live in.

Bull sharks help to keep the populations of fish and marine animals balanced.

Size

Bull sharks often grow to be between 7 and 11.5 feet long. The longest bull shark found was over 13 feet long.

They usually weigh between 200 and 300 pounds, but have been known to weigh over 500 pounds.

Like many other sharks, female

bull sharks are larger than male

bull sharks.

Bull sharks are wider than many other sharks. They have a short, blunt snout and small eyes.

Like other sharks, bull sharks have gills on the sides of their body. The gills take in oxygen from the water so they can breathe.

Bull sharks use their coloring for **camouflage**. The white belly blends in with the ocean surface, and the dark top blends in with darker waters.

7

Habitat

Bull sharks are found in warm, tropical waters. They are often found around the **coastline** in more shallow water.

Bull sharks have been known to swim up rivers and into lakes. They are the only kind of shark to be able to live in salt water and freshwater.

Bull sharks are found in the Atlantic, Pacific, and Indian oceans.

They have also been found in the Amazon river, Mississippi river, and Lake Nicaragua.

■■

Diet

Bull sharks are **carnivores**. They only eat meat.

Their diet is made up of fish, sea turtles, sting rays, sea birds, and dolphins. They have also been known to eat other sharks, including other bull sharks.

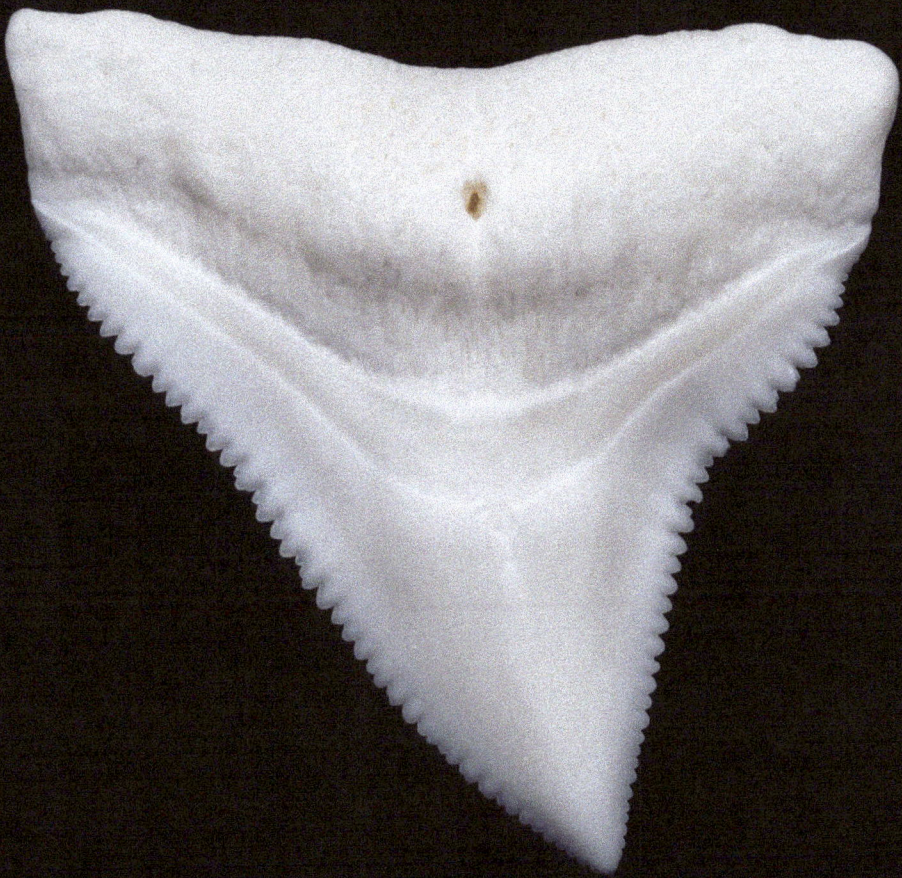

Bull shark teeth have a **serrated** edge. They have little grooves that help the shark to tear their food.

13

Bull sharks do something called "bump and bite" to catch their prey. They start by bumping, or running into, their prey to stun it. Then, once they have bumped into it, they eat it.

Bull sharks have a very good sense of smell. They are able to smell injured prey from far away.

They are also able to detect electrical fields with special pores on their snout. This is very helpful in dark waters.

Shark Attacks

Bull sharks are known to be **aggressive**. While they do not hunt humans, they are known to attack swimmers who get too close.

They may also mistake humans for prey. Many divers do not swim near bull sharks for this reason.

Bull sharks are thought to be one of the most dangerous sharks to humans because they are so **aggressive**.

Movement

Bull sharks are often seen swimming slowly along the ocean floor. However, their size and shape allows them to swim fast for short bursts.

They have been seen swimming at speeds of almost 12 miles per hour when chasing prey.

Bull sharks are rarely seen near the ocean surface. They usually swim closer to the ocean floor.

Bull Shark Pups

Bull sharks have a **brood** of up to 13 babies, or pups. Their pups are usually born near rivers where the water is less salty. This keeps pups safe from larger sharks.

Pups are usually between two and three feet long when they are born.

Bull sharks stay around where

they were born for the first four

or five years of their lives.

Bull Shark Life

Bull sharks are usually **solitary**. They spend most of their time alone. They are sometimes seen in small groups, or schools.

Some bull sharks have been seen traveling long distances. Females return to the same place every time they have pups.

While bull sharks usually hunt alone, they will sometimes come together in an area with lots of prey.

Freshwater Sharks

Bull sharks have a special **ability** that allows them to swim in freshwater.

They have a special gland near their tail that helps them **regulate** the salt in their body. Their kidneys also help them to **regulate** the salt.

Bull sharks live in the freshwater

of Lake Nicaragua in Central

America.

Population

Bull sharks are listed as **near threatened**. Their populations are **declining** in many parts of the world.

If their population continues **declining**, it is possible that they could become **endangered.**

Bull sharks often live between ten and sixteen years. They may live as long as 30 years in **captivity**.

Bull Sharks in Danger

Bull sharks are often affected by pollution as they spend a lot of time close to the coast. They are also affected by human activity along the coast.

They are hunted for their meat, hides, oil, and fins. In parts of Asia, their fins are used to make shark fin soup.

Many bull sharks are caught by mistake when people are catching fish with nets.

Helping Bull Sharks

Many groups are researching bull sharks to get a better understanding of how they can be helped.

Scientists use satellite tags to track sharks. Knowing where and when sharks go is important for being able to help them.

People working to prevent pollution and remove trash from the ocean. This can help bull sharks and other ocean animals.

In some countries, there are laws that prevent sharks from being hunted for their fins. There are also laws about fishing methods to help prevent sharks being caught by mistake.

Glossary

Ability: the power to do something

Aggressive: mean, ready to fight or attack

Apex predator: the top predator in a food chain

Brood: animals born at the same time

Camouflage: using color to blend in to the surroundings

Captivity: animals that are kept by humans, not in the wild

Carnivore: an animal that eats only meat

Coastline: the area of land along the water

Declining: getting smaller

Ecosystem: living things and the area they live in

Endangered: at risk of extinction

Near threatened: when a population of an animal is getting closer to becoming endangered

Predator: an animal that hunts other animals for food

Regulate: to control, adjust

Serrated: having grooves or notches

Solitary: living alone

About the Author

Victoria Blakemore is a first grade

teacher in Southwest Florida with a

passion for reading.

You can visit her at

www.elementaryexplorers.com

Also in This Series

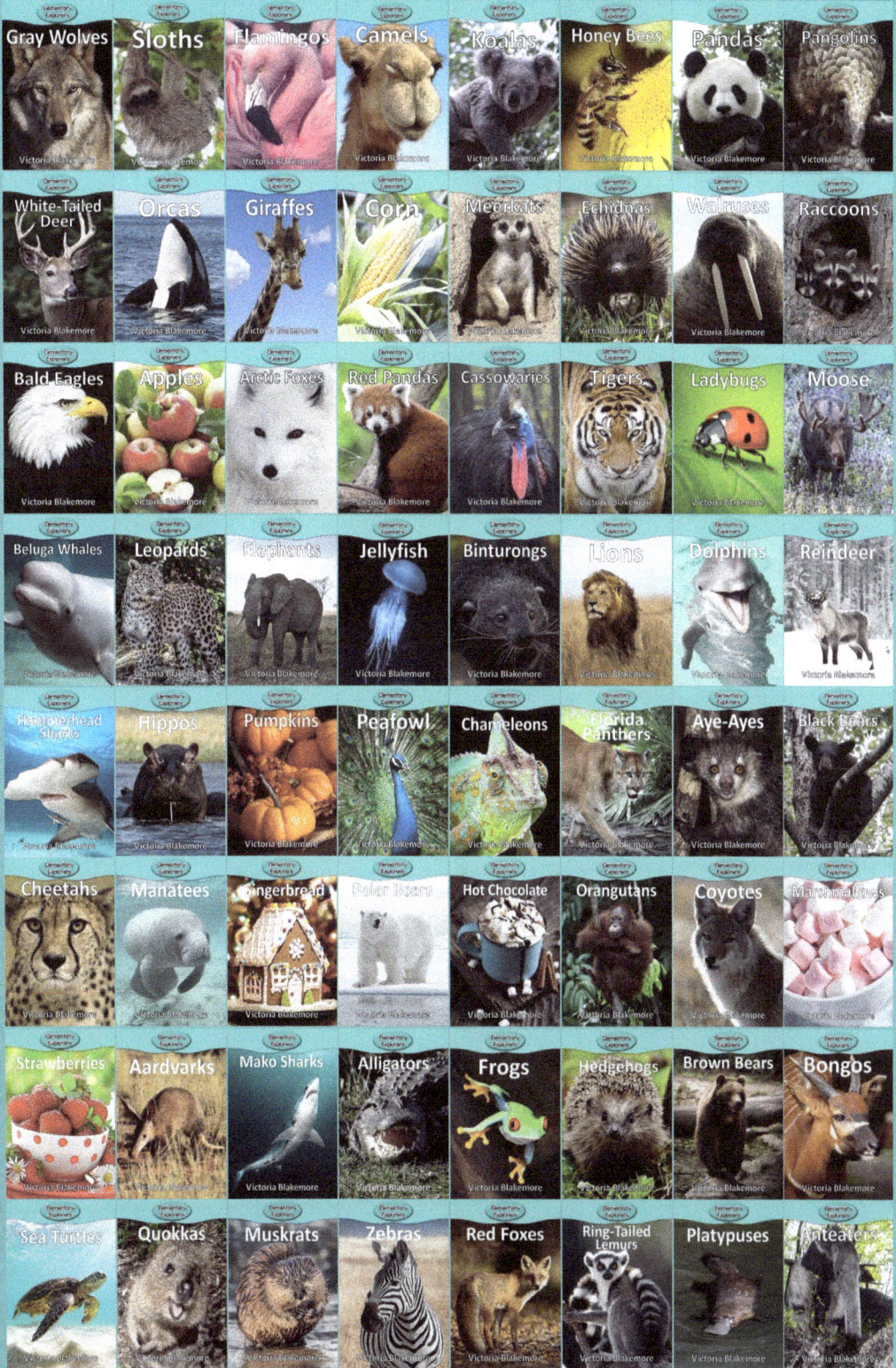

Gray Wolves	Sloths	Flamingos	Camels	Koalas	Honey Bees	Pandas	Pangolins
White-Tailed Deer	Orcas	Giraffes	Corn	Meerkats	Echidnas	Walruses	Raccoons
Bald Eagles	Apples	Arctic Foxes	Red Pandas	Cassowaries	Tigers	Ladybugs	Moose
Beluga Whales	Leopards	Elephants	Jellyfish	Binturongs	Lions	Dolphins	Reindeer
Hammerhead Sharks	Hippos	Pumpkins	Peafowl	Chameleons	Florida Panthers	Aye-Ayes	Black Bears
Cheetahs	Manatees	Gingerbread	Polar Bears	Hot Chocolate	Orangutans	Coyotes	Marshmallows
Strawberries	Aardvarks	Mako Sharks	Alligators	Frogs	Hedgehogs	Brown Bears	Bongos
Sea Turtles	Quokkas	Muskrats	Zebras	Red Foxes	Ring-Tailed Lemurs	Platypuses	Anteaters

Victoria Blakemore

Also in This Series

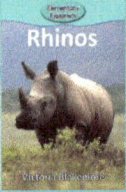

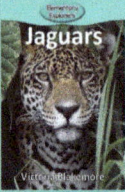

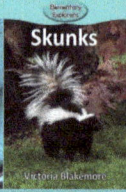

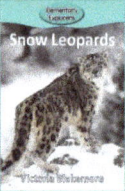

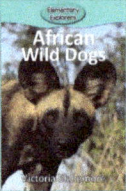

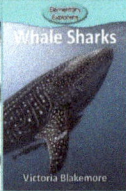

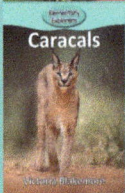

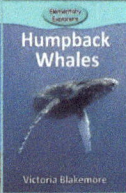

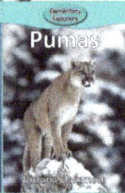

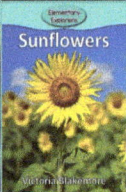

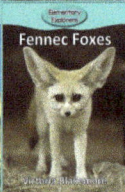

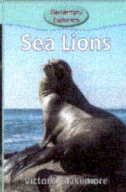

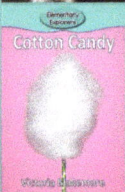

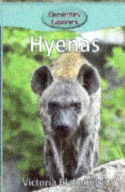

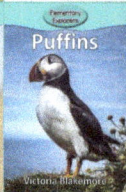

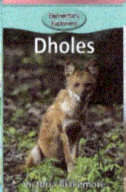

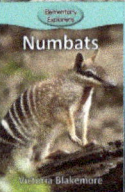

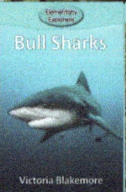

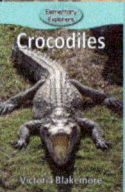

Kangaroos · Rhinos · Jaguars · Wombats · Capybaras · Gorillas · Cats · Skunks

Butterflies · Dingoes · Snow Leopards · African Wild Dogs · Penguins · Whale Sharks · Wolverines · Warthogs

Caracals · Badgers · Seals · Hummingbirds · Pikas · Humpback Whales · Pumas · Lemonade

Llamas · Tulips · Ostriches · Sunflowers · Fennec Foxes · Sea Lions · Squirrels · Roses

Porcupines · Ice Cream · Cotton Candy · Chocolate · Hyenas · Toucans · Saigas · Puffins

Doughnuts · Dholes · Kudus · Ocelots · Numbats · Bull Sharks · Crocodiles

Victoria Blakemore

www.ingramcontent.com/pod-product-compliance
Lightning Source LLC
Chambersburg PA
CBHW042248040426
42335CB00043B/3107